TRUE STATEMENTS SPOKEN BY UNBELIEVERS

PAUL D. KACSUR

TRUE STATEMENTS SPOKEN BY UNBELIEVERS

Heathens Say The Darnedest Things

ReadersMagnet, LLC

CONTENTS

INTRODUCTION

Scriptural biographies record people's deeds at their best or worst, warts and all. A few of these statements were selected for this volume. These words spoken by unbelievers reveal truths that Christians know are immutable as explained in Scripture. People with different belief systems other than Scriptural-based teachings do stumble onto Biblical truth occasionally. Winston Churchill said, *"Men do stumble across the truth once in a while, but they usually pick themselves up and brush off, continuing as if nothing happened."* This is a common human tendency when it comes to Scriptural truth. These accounts are from various types of literature in both Testaments.

The Lord's truth is all around us. We live in the midst of it. We see life experiences continually verify the truth of God as explained in Scripture. Many miss God's truth, so this book notes a few remarkable exceptions.

The true statements referred to here are surprising, especially when we see who said them. People unknowingly declare truth, not realizing their words are compatible with Scripture, confirming truths revealed throughout the Bible. They are recorded primarily as accurate history but also for our edification and learning. At the same time, they can be quite amusing. Notice how these stories unfold bringing us to these statements made by unbelievers. If we know Scripture and the essence of God's Word and if we live with our eyes and ears open, we might hear similar statements today. May the Lord continually be blessed and honored by statements of truth, regardless of who says it, whatever their intentions.

King Darius Says to Daniel:

"YOUR GOD WILL DELIVER YOU"

--–◦≈◦–--

We don't realize how closely people watch us. We leave an impact on others. We are being watched closer than we think. The Prophet Daniel is a prime example of this, seen here by how King Darius observed his life. Daniel was among those carried away in the Babylonian captivity, a bad time in Israel's history. The Israelite exiles had orders not to worship any other God, especially the One True God of Israel. Laws of the Medes and Persians were deemed unchangeable and everyone knew it. This particular law was enacted for spite, on purpose, just to seize the devoted exile Daniel.

The thing with Daniel and the faithful of Israel was that they would not bow to another god or king. The Babylonian officials knew that. When Daniel was appointed as one of the governors, those who knew of his faithfulness wanted to frame him. They were not able to find "any fault or error" in him (v. 4). They knew the only way they could get him was to find some connection to the God Daniel daily worshipped. Daniel's faith was *that dependable* and predictable. Verse 5 reveals their intent: "*...we shall not find any charge against this Daniel unless we find it against him concerning the law of his God.*"

That is quite a statement concerning Daniel's faithfulness. Daniel was what we would call a "straight shooter." They could find nothing questionable or crooked to accuse him, and by observing Daniel's constant dedication to his God, they knew he would remain faithful.

Consequently, the captors devised a new law, which stated: to no other deity could prayer be directed except to King Darius. If anyone broke that law, he'd be thrown into the lion's den. The law could not be changed. It was the "Law of the Medes and Persians." They thought they had Daniel trapped. They knew Daniel's faithfulness to the One True God would not be shaken. The law would find *that fault* in him…and it did.

Daniel heard the law, went home and prayed three times daily as usual. Nothing changed in his commitment to the Lord. The enemies of God intended to find Daniel praying and they did. They immediately went to tell the King. It sounds like they tattled on him. "Oh, King Darius, Daniel is breaking your new law and *now* you have to throw him into the lion's den…"

The King did not like this and tried to determine a way out of this situation for Daniel. Pagan kings like Darius usually wouldn't get emotionally involved with victims, but there was something different about Daniel and his "excellent spirit." This situation involving Daniel bothered Darius deeply. The accusers approached the King and reminded him of the immutability of his law—it could not be changed. "It's the law and you made it." It's like they were saying, "King, you have to do this and we don't care if you don't like it."

This brings us to the true statement spoken by a heathen king. Darius, reluctantly condemning Daniel made the following compassionate-sounding faith-based statement of truth. Listen to his empathy as he says to Daniel, "*Your God, Whom you serve continually will deliver you.*" This wasn't some lame confirmation to someone else's religion. People usually don't care what others believe but this was different. Daniel's faithfulness made an impression upon this king. Nevertheless, Daniel was reluctantly condemned by the king because of the law he was tricked into making so these men could condemn Daniel.

How did it work out for the accusers? Watch this: The next day after no food and a sleepless night, the king went down to the den into which Daniel had been thrown to be devoured by lions. The king *cried out with a lamenting voice...*" Sounds like uncertainty, which was totally to be expected in a situation like this. What does Darius hear in response? Daniel's voice came forth answering the king respectively that all was well and that God had *sent His angel to shut the mouths of the lions.*

The king was relieved and immediately made plans for those who plotted against Daniel. These men, their wives and children were thrown into that same den. The Biblical text says all their bones were broken before their bodies reached the bottom of the den. That sounds horrifying. Have you ever seen lions feeding at the zoo, crunching bones as if they were twigs?

Miracles like this divine deliverance and intervention call for a finish like this. As it was with the sin of Achan recorded in the book of Joshua, because of this sin against Daniel entire families paid the price. Liberal anti-Scripture critics say this was no miracle. They presume the lions were either tamed, toothless, or just not hungry. This dramatic end proved that was not the case.

What else can be said of such a clear testimony that rings true? We want to rejoice with Daniel and march in his victory parade.

The question is, would we be willing to stand with him as he was condemned for his faith? If any of us ever enjoy a victory as this, there will be a price to be paid first. That price would be one of resolve and faith to stand firm even when our lives are on the line.

> *Dare to be a Daniel, Dare to stand alone.*
> *Dare to have a purpose sure, and dare to make it known.*

Ahab saying to Jehoshaphat:

"HE NEVER PROPHESIES GOOD ABOUT ME."

This is about someone who doesn't want to hear the truth. Ever met anyone like that? Micaiah, a genuine prophet of the Lord was sought out by King Jehoshaphat as he and King Ahab planned a military attack. Micaiah was asked for guidance even though he was hated by King Ahab. This is not unusual for people to avoid uncomfortable truths if they can. Zedekiah, one of Ahab's "prophets," preached an illustrated message of victory to Ahab, using cattle horns to stress his point. "This is how you will win the battle and gore your enemies," Zedekiah said. His message was a lie.

As Micaiah was brought from jail, the men who retrieved him told him to go along with what the others prophesied. "Come on," they said, "just agree with them and everything will be fine." This is still a popular way to gloss over important teachings of Scripture. We prefer to go along to get along. His reply in verse 14 is one we should remember: "*...whatever the Lord says to me that will I speak.*" Micaiah would speak the truth, *no matter what.*

The genuine prophet Micaiah was a unique sort of Bible character. He had a biting sense of humor too. When King Ahab and Jehoshaphat asked him if they should go to war, he said, "Go and prosper...the Lord will deliver you..." This is exactly what Ahab wanted to hear, but *he knew it wasn't the truth.* What happened next is puzzling. Ahab rebuked Micaiah saying "How many times have I told you to tell me nothing but the truth in the Name of the Lord?" Micaiah then tells him, "I saw Israel scattered like sheep with no shepherd." The image of Israel's king as a shepherd is a familiar one. His message was that Ahab would be killed and Israel scattered. So, what did Ahab say? His statement of truth came as he complained to Jehoshaphat about the faithful prophet: "*Didn't I tell you he wouldn't prophesy good about me?*" Exactly what he didn't want to hear was what he complained about not hearing (?) Running from the truth makes people act strange.

Micaiah then unloads the whole truth on the wicked king (verses 19-23). How did Zedekiah, the false prophet take this? He smacked Micaiah, and with a tone of sarcastic blasphemy asked, "*Which way the Spirit of the Lord is moving…?*" That's how he took it. This is another expression of how people racked with guilt and conviction deal with truth. They lash out, even physically attacking those who oppose them because they can't handle the truth. Micaiah's reply was simple and powerful: "You will see on that day when you go into an inner chamber to hide yourself." This doesn't sound like a peaceful outcome for King Ahab, and it wasn't.

Ahab had Micaiah thrown back into jail, sounding like an ancient version of solitary confinement, eating bread and drinking the water of affliction. Ahab's final presumptuous words to the prophet sound confident: "... *until I return in peace.*" That meant, in Ahab's deluded mind, all would be well and he would live through this battle. Micaiah's words are the final verdict of this situation: **"If you ever return in peace, the Lord has not spoken by me... Take heed all you people."** This final stab from the prophet echoes Moses' standard explaining how people know who the real prophets are. This standard for true prophets is found in Deuteronomy 18:21-22. Prophets are judged by their words and whether their prophesies actually happen. Some in Micaiah's audience knew of that reference. It was the legitimate method to verify a prophet and they knew it.

Micaiah was right. Ahab was killed and the dogs licked his blood just as Elijah prophesied. The place where the dogs licked the blood of Ahab was also a place where harlots bathed. That could have taken place simultaneously. King Ahab was a spiritual harlot because he was an idolater. Therefore, his demise and death is associated with harlots.

This is a fascinating and entertaining story, but moderns may wonder what the implications are for us. What does a story like this have to do with my life?

We live, move and have our being sustained by truth from Scripture, our all-sufficient rule of faith and practice. By and through Scripture we know what is real. However, we are like sheep and are easily deceived. Voices clamoring for attention tell us to believe this or follow that. *How do we know what is right?* The correct answers come as we verify everything through God's infallible Word. This is the truth, especially if we don't want to hear it or it doesn't say nice things about how we live. Ever been around someone offended by a Bible message? They get irritated. Likewise, we don't enjoy hearing things that run counter to how *we think* things should be. We like others to agree with us or, at the very least, would rather have them leave us alone to do what we want. We do not operate as this historical narrative explains, but the principle is the same: We stand by the Word of God and some don't want to hear it.

In our day, absolute truth is not announced through a Prophet like Elijah or Micaiah, but through precise interpretation of Scripture. A modern version of how some don't want to hear truth may be helpful. This is a true story:

A young man was called to preach but was not yet a pastor. He found places where people gathered, whether on street corners or any public place. He decided to preach to a holiday-weekend crowd at a river resort in the Texas Hill Country. People flock to places like this for long weekends and vacations. The preacher, while standing in the middle of a shallow river, (on State property) shouted the Gospel from a homemade sheet metal megaphone. After about 15-20 minutes, an owner of one the camping spots came running down the hill to the river. As he bounded down the hill, he screamed frantically, *"Shut up, shut up! I'm telling you, shut up."* The guy was irate. He ran wild-eyed and crazy, right up to the young preacher's face and proclaimed these true words: *"You, shut up! I've got people renting spaces up here doing things they are not supposed to be doing, and I don't want you telling them about it!"*

What causes a person to have such a violent reaction to the Gospel? It could be he was worried about losing money. This could happen if people responded to the preaching, ruining his business. People are still the same as Ahab. In some cases, they don't want others to hear the truth, especially if it causes one to lose money. We need to trust in the Word of God to guide us through whatever comes our way in whatever time we have left here on earth. It's getting later than you think.

Pharaoh Saying to Moses:

"BLESS ME ALSO"

People want God's blessings without a personal relationship with Him. Unbelievers know there is something to the grace and favor resting on God's children and they desire *a piece of it*. Just a piece—not all that cross bearing and self-denial, just the blessing part. It is possible to know about the Lord and want His blessings but not want Jesus with all that He requires. This is a common way of thinking: *blessings without commitment*. Dedication to the Lord might cramp one's style. It's not our style or comfort with which the Lord is concerned but rather that His plans work through us. Recently the U.S. Marines had an advertising campaign reminding us why this elite fighting force is so effective. The billboard said: "We don't accept applications, only commitments." God's plans also do not come without commitment on our part. After commitment, blessings do follow. Some however, want a short cut.

We consider Pharaoh to be an obstinate bully, one whose heart God had hardened as Pharaoh himself added to the process becoming even more hard-hearted. This Bible passage chronologically places us right after the last plague and death of the firstborn. Pharaoh finally let God's people go. We wonder what took so long. He could have responded to Moses earlier and spared his firstborn son. Pharaoh was stubborn, unteachable and authoritative. This is the guy who was asked by Moses when he wanted him to get rid of the frogs and he answered, "Tomorrow." A plague of frogs stunk and Pharaoh was content to wait until the next day? Who in their right mind would wait until tomorrow while sitting with the man connected with the King of the universe Who has the power to remove the plague?

There are interesting correlations of this bizarre choice with how some people choose to live with situations, which keep them from spiritual victories. Some of these things stink too. Yet, we say when faced with powerful and glorious victories that are so close, "Tomorrow." Sometimes tomorrow stretches into years *or never happens.*

By this part of the story, Pharaoh was fed up with the Israelites. He wasn't totally against this all-powerful One True God of the Israelites that he abused for so long. He did recognize there could be something in it for him. This is why, as he grudgingly let God's people go, he issued this order to Moses, "… *bless me also.*" Here we see an unbeliever with enough faith to ask for a personal blessing. This has to make one wonder about the nerve of this guy. Before we judge him, look at us. Who do we think we are to ignore God's commandments, be cruel to His covenant people (Israel), and then have the audacity to ask for His blessings? Today most politicians end their speeches with "God bless America." Yet in their political stance they could be against Israel, …but still ask for a blessing from this same God of Israel. What nerve!

Pharaoh was a harsh slave driver, ever increasing the workload on his Hebrew slaves but wanting their God to bless him? Often people with great power have delusions, supposing all the world revolves around their desires. Mad men like Hitler, Hussein, and Muammar Gaddafi had such delusions.

This type of unbridled nerve is called *chutzpah*, an interesting Yiddish word. The "chu" is pronounced as if clearing the back of your throat. A simple illustration explains: A boy who killed both his parents was being sentenced. After being found guilty, he asked the judge to have mercy and let him off without penalty *because he was now an orphan*. That's chutzpah! Pharaoh's asking for a blessing from Moses' God was like that. Who did he think he was? Do we find this strange?

We moderns have nerve also. We express it in various circumstances. Consider what we see in church with *CEO's*. These are not corporate executives. These CEO's attend church on *C*hristmas and *E*aster *o*nly. Some feel entitled to God's blessings while the majority of the year they ignore His commandments. Still they'll say in a rare church appearance, "...*bless me also*."

That's chutzpah!

Unmarried people living together sometimes ask for a church wedding. There may be no mention or even consideration of repentance or a willingness to stop their open life of sin. What difference do we think a church ceremony makes when our lives ignore God's supremacy and commandments? Some examples could be even worse in liberal churches which do not rely on Scripture for God's marital authority. People ignore God but still say, "...bless me also." Again, that's chutzpah!

Many people today ignore God's commandments on tithing or being involved with financial support for Kingdom endeavors (church-related business). Then when faced with a money crisis, we call on the Lord to help us through the situation. The Lord just might help us too. Our better-than-good God is like that. He gives people space and grace to repent and change for the better.

The people with money issues may not have plans to make things right about tithing or giving anything to their church, but they still want God's blessings on their lives. Their life might be a hedonistic, idolatrous, covetous lifestyle, centered primarily around selfish interests and material wealth. Yet, they have the nerve to say, "…bless me also." Is that right? No, it's chutzpah!

Prevalent thinking outside church circles is even worse. Many presume that most people go to Heaven without ever consulting God's plan, but they still say, "bless me also." Recently people have been using the phrase "have a blessed day" instead of the usual "good day." Ever ask those offering that nice benefit what they mean? They might be referring to the blessing from an Elton John song for all we know. We never know unless we ask, but you can expect various sources of "blessing" outside those described in Scripture.

It's easy to look down on Pharaoh and judge him. He was an evil person. Pharaoh knows the truth now, but how blind are we to our own audacity and sense of heavenly entitlement? We don't want to admit it but self-discipline and self-denial are difficult. We keep working on it regardless of where we are in the process. Our God does desire to bless us, but He deserves better from His servants. Those servants should be us.

Naaman says to Elisha:

"ARE NOT ABANAH AND PHARPAR BETTER RIVERS?"

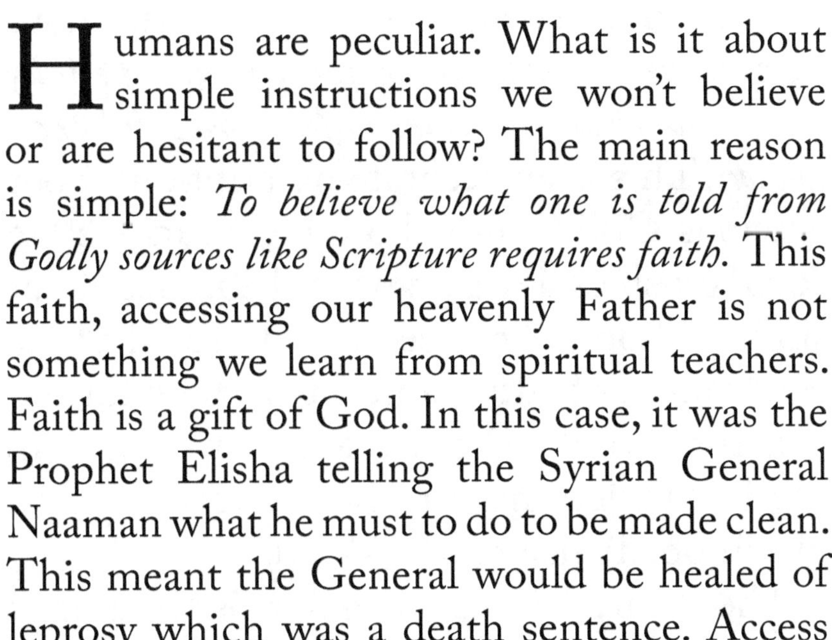

Humans are peculiar. What is it about simple instructions we won't believe or are hesitant to follow? The main reason is simple: *To believe what one is told from Godly sources like Scripture requires faith.* This faith, accessing our heavenly Father is not something we learn from spiritual teachers. Faith is a gift of God. In this case, it was the Prophet Elisha telling the Syrian General Naaman what he must to do to be made clean. This meant the General would be healed of leprosy which was a death sentence. Access to a genuine man of God meant there was hope for a miracle.

Consider this story of Elisha and Naaman, rarely appreciated by outsiders to the faith. Many people take the Word of God for granted, mostly ignoring it. The man of God Elisha instructs a General, one who was probably used to special treatment because of his high rank. People of rank and stature usually are treated differently. Suddenly the General was taking orders from a prophet. What happened was *an act of grace and mercy.* A loving God acted magnanimously through one of His servants. To be magnanimous means *very generous or forgiving, especially toward a rival or someone less powerful than oneself.* This is an accurate description of our gracious God. *This* is how He treats us. He could crush us like a grape in the midst of our sin but chooses to save us and use what He can from our faulty frame. He is merciful and generous to all who are less powerful than He is. We just have to honor His way and live in obedience to His Word.

The heart of this chapter is Naaman's statement, which was true. His reply to

Elisha came as a question: "Aren't the rivers in Damascus, the Abanah and the Pharpar, better than all Israel's waters? Couldn't I wash in them and get clean?" The rivers he mentions really were better than the muddy Jordan river where Elisha told him to go. On the surface they were better rivers, or so he thought. One of our problems is that we think too much. The rivers Naaman mentioned were beautiful rivers—one known for watering orchards and gardens as it flowed from the mountains of Damascus.

The problem with our opinions and life observations is that they cause us to stumble over obvious truth in Scripture. This was the case with Naaman. "Look at how much better these rivers are." The fact of which river looks better doesn't matter when God sends us somewhere else. Notice how people will do any number of things if they think it somehow makes them appear right. There are many expressions of "works-righteousness" and there always have been. Prideful man usually seeks a path to DIY (do it yourself), even for impossible spiritual endeavors like the salvation of our soul.

The instructions were not difficult. Naaman went to Elisha's house, but after arriving things didn›t go the way Naaman anticipated. Elisha the prophet didn't even come out to greet him. Instead, Elisha sent his messenger with the formula for a miracle. This story has been called "seven ducks in a dirty river" because of the simple instructions: "Go wash in the Jordan seven times." The General got upset that the prophet didn't show up to at least wave his hand over the leprosy or do something, anything. Instead, he sends him to a dirty river! Who treats a general like that? That is when Naaman's question entered and what he said was the truth. Remember this: True observations do not matter when it comes to how God does something. *Our logic fails when God's plans are otherwise.* After Naaman left mad, even his servants knew he should at least try it. Their advice and rationale for simple obedience should be a model for anyone who stumbles over the simplicity of the Gospel. The servants said to Naaman, "Why don't you try it? What do you have to lose? If the prophet told you some complicated set of acts you had to accomplish, you would do it, wouldn't you?" All it would take was just seven dunks—in the right river.

Naaman decided to obey what the prophet said and came out of the Jordan river healed from his leprosy. Naaman went back to Elisha's house (about 25 miles) and acknowledged, "…there is no God (like the God of Elisha) in all the earth…" This is a great statement for anyone to announce, even if they are still held captive to a life of sin. It is the only acceptable thing to say. We don't know the condition of Naaman's heart at that point. His stating that there is only one God did however put the Israelites to shame. They were the ones who should have known that about the Lord. They blasphemously believed that both the Lord God of Israel and Baal (a pagan deity) were gods. This was not all inhabitants in Israel, but some. Humans are easily led astray. This confession of One True God is a big deal, especially for the one making it. This is what the Lord desires to hear. He doesn't need alternative methods or multiple gods to assist Him with His eternal plans. *When people interject modifications into God's plans, nothing is right.* The Almighty doesn't need our help.

The lesson to learn from this story is that secular people object to the simplicity of the Gospel. People think there *must be* something more than what Scripture says. We like religion. We like complicated rites and ceremonies relying on our accomplishments (about which we can brag) to do right or make us feel better. We like praise for our deeds, no matter how insignificant in this life here and now. God wants us to have the best later when treasure lasts forever. There's just One Door to eternal life—Jesus Christ. This story reminds us how wrong it is for people to presume they can rationally negotiate with God. Let us take God at His Word and believe what He tells us on how to be free—free indeed!

Nebuchadnezzar says to the witnesses:

"THE FOURTH IS LIKE THE SON OF GOD"

In the chapter regarding Daniel and the lion's den, King Darius declared a public dedication to the mighty God of Israel. This chapter reveals another declaration made by a different heathen king, Nebuchadnezzar. In spite of enduring fiery trials and when acting for righteousness' sake, it is possible that the Lord goes through the fire with us. This miraculous event has encouraged believers throughout history.

Some scholars have suggested Nebuchadnezzar's statement meant he saw a manifestation of a pagan god in the burning furnace with the three young Hebrew men. It is unlikely he thought that. The reason the three were thrown into the fire was because of their faithful allegiance to the One True God of Israel. They didn't bow to any lesser god, they didn't bow down when commanded to; and as everyone saw, they didn't burn either. But, and this is significant, when they were thrown into the fire, they had no guarantee their God would deliver them. Imagine thinking this might be it… and what a horrible end that would be. The soldiers who threw them into the furnace perished from getting close to the raging fire, heated seven times more than usual. You have to think of how terrifying that was. We know this story is accurate because we know the dependability of Scripture. Those faithful Hebrew men didn't know when the end would come for their lives or how dreadful it could be.

We pay special attention to the Hebrew men's final statement of faith (or what they thought was their final words): "*Our God is able to deliver us…* They knew this was true. The more amazing part of their statement was this: *…**But if he doesn't…***"The interesting thing about those words was that they were not only caring for their safety. Neither was this a one-way confession, meaning it would only result in their benefit. We love prayers like that. The thing about some modern confessions or statements of faith is that our words usually have us in the position of victory. We tend to pray like that. This story is so different because these men left the results up to God. *That is faith.*

So, who was that extra one in the fire? This was *their Lord*, the One *they trusted* in the fire with them. Some have called the fourth the Lord's angel. Either way, this was a manifestation of God's saving grace for His Name's sake. It is unlikely that a pagan god came to the rescue for these Jewish men's faithfulness to the One True God. Add also to this event, pagan false gods do not have power as does the Lord or His servants. Yet that does not stop people from making up nonsensical reasons for what we see happening. It seems some will gravitate toward any explanation that excludes the One True God and Father of our Lord Jesus Christ.

We mention this account because if we are one of God's faithful as these men were, our God is with us as He was with the three in the fire. We may not realize it and others may not make a declaration of the Lord accompanying us through the trial, but that doesn't mean He is not with us. We shouldn't expect heathens to notice God's intervention in our lives anyway. They usually notice when *it seems* like the Lord is not with us, even though we know He always is. If you read this recognizing the Lord's providential watch-care, consider yourself fortunate to hear such a confession from the young men's lips and understand what it took for them to say that. We use their words on that occasion to further a witness for His glory. We have to listen closely because it is a rare event that the ungodly see God's great protective care over us. Then again, even a blind squirrel finds a nut once in a while. We must pay attention to the confession of these three: They knew their God was able to deliver them (3:18 ff). That is the main thing. *Whether He chose to deliver them or not, the faithful left it up to Him.*

As far as unbelievers thinking God is not with us, we are more accustomed to hear ignorant observers say something like: "The man upstairs is mad at you." They use this excuse for whatever bad things they see happen to us. Such ignorant comments should be ignored by God's people. We know better. How many of us can say as we were in the midst of a trial that we sensed His presence with us? It would be nice to have our heathen friends or family notice that He is with us, but whether they do or not, that doesn't mean He is not there. We know He is.

The big question is: who was this in the fire with the Hebrews? Conservative scholarship agrees this was a preincarnate appearance of our Lord Jesus Christ. There are several occasions where Jesus may have appeared in the Old Testament and this is probably the case. It could also have been an angel; but knowing our Lord and His care for His people, it is not a stretch of the imagination that it was the Lord Himself. That the ungodly didn't know for sure doesn't take away from this miracle. That won Nebuchadnezzar over in his thinking about true divinity. Notice his response after the miracle. Read 3:28ff: "Blessed be the God of Shadrach, Meshach and Abed-Nego, who sent His Angel and delivered His servants who trusted in Him…" That became holy ground.

"THESE MEN ARE SERVANTS OF THE MOST HIGH GOD"

Here is an example requiring discernment and a leading of the Holy Spirit. We have someone here who spoke the truth, but there was a disturbing difference. Here is a case when truth spoken by a faulty vessel is not praiseworthy. The interesting thing here is that what she said was absolutely true: *"These men are the servants of the Most High God, who proclaim to us the way of salvation."* What is wrong with saying that? That depends on who says it. Nevertheless, we enjoy praiseworthy words about us especially when it has to do with our ministry. Who wouldn't want some positive buzz? This went on for many days. We don't know how many, but eventually it disturbed the Apostle Paul and it had to stop.

Luke, the author of this historical account, tells us the girl who spoke those true words was possessed with a spirit of divination. The literal translation of what she had was a *python spirit*. This comes from Greek mythology. Essentially this girl was a medium in contact with demons who could supposedly predict the future. We don't know how accurate her predictions were but they must have been good enough to turn a profit for her masters. Large profits do not mean the money was made ethically or that what was sold was worth it. They were condemned spiritual activities. There are no just practices using divination. God is not impressed nor does He approve.

As it is with other historical accounts, we wish we knew more about this situation. Why and how did the occurrence eventually involve Paul? What is so wrong with people proclaiming a genuine ministry? The Apostle

Paul was for real. Ministries like his were as legitimate as they come. Why did the Apostle get fed up with the girl's endorsement? We're not told why. We are however, told how long it took to finally shut her up. He (Paul the Apostle) cast out her source of demonic information and she was delivered and clean within the hour.

We must understand this: The Most High God, rightly referred to as such, does not need demonic endorsements to further His glorious cause. He has used donkeys to get His message across when needed. Jesus told us praise was so intricate to His ministry that if people didn't praise Him, rocks would cry out. This actually happens today as rocks testify to Scriptural truth as archeologists and geologists do their research. We might suppose that the source of praise for ministry is not that critical. This girl inspired by a bad spirit was another pagan voice telling the truth. The problem was that this true statement came from a faulty source. We don't need demonic endorsements and neither did Paul. God would rather have inanimate rocks praising Him rather than demons.

There are times when accolades—words of praise or flattery—do not add to our mission. There are times when empty praise is more of a distraction rather than a verification of true ministry. We are not told the details but we understand it had to stop.

At some point Paul became so annoyed with the chatter that he turned and spoke to the spirit. He didn't speak to the girl. He addressed the source of her information and commanded it to come out of her. We're told the spirit came out that very hour. Again, we'd like to know more particulars about how this took place so that we might pattern exorcisms to work as effectively. We are not told those details. What we are told is the consequence or fallout from her masters. That seemed to be the central concern. Those men were upset because the Apostle Paul ended their money-making enterprise.

Make sure you understand how the events unfolded. A demon was cast out of a girl and her masters were upset because that hurt their business. All they cared about was money. Sound familiar? They didn't care that her utterances were correct and that Paul and Silas were indeed servants of the Most High God. They just saw their hopes for profit were ended, well, with that person anyway.

Consequently, Paul and Silas were dragged into the marketplace and accused of troubling the city. Just the fact of their being Jews added to their accusers' sour attitudes. The magistrates commanded they be beaten with rods and thrown into prison. Antisemitism is not a new hate crime. This was their immediate reward for being servants of the Most High God. Doesn't sound right, does it? Shouldn't they have been honored and blessed? Wasn't there any recognition of the bad spirit which had just been cast out of the girl? Wasn't that a good thing? Well, not when it affects profits. Gospel freedom often takes a back seat when money is involved. We are reminded again that this world system is driven by the popular false god—money.

The main thing here is just because someone speaks truth concerning the Gospel or a ministry, that doesn't mean God endorses it. May God give us wisdom to know the difference.

"I KNOW WHO YOU ARE, THE HOLY ONE OF GOD"

At times, we see amazing things happen in the spiritual realm. One of these things is when people, whether losing touch with reality or influenced by a demonic source claim to be either Jesus or the devil. Whether these accounts are legitimate or not must be examined, preferably with a case study of that person's mental records. In these Biblical events, we are told exactly what the diagnosis is. There was no question about mental health. Here in both accounts the problem was clearly demonic.

The first account takes place in the synagogue where Jesus taught. People noticed

His authoritative style and were astonished. He was so unlike the scribes. The narrative gets interesting as we see a guy in that church service who had an unclean spirit. We don't know how a person with that dark influence could be in church but that is a lesson for us today. Listen to what he says (and imagine the disruption in the service). He cries out addressing Jesus and says, "*Let us alone! What have we to do with You, Jesus of Nazareth? Did You come to destroy us? I know Who You are… the Holy One of God.*"

That proclamation shows us several things, besides the true statement from a demon. First of all, people with dark demonic power can attend church. We like to think everybody in a church service is right with the Lord, but you never know. Maybe that guy was there all the time, but when Jesus showed up and taught with authority, that brings out the best or the worst in people.

Not only can there be bad people in church, but when confronted with anointed teaching through the Spirit of God, that spiritual setting can bring about a reaction.

In this account, the demon cried out and identified Jesus correctly. That's the second thing: Demons have an accurate Christology. Within systematic theological disciplines, Christology is the formal study of the Person and work of the Lord Jesus Christ. It is through this study we know Who Jesus is: the Holy One of God.

That wasn't all the demon had right. Not only did the demon correctly identify Jesus, but he also knew about future events concerning the ungodly. Demons know it is only a matter of time before Jesus ends all satanic deception. Demons know about the end times as foretold in Scripture. They know their days are numbered.

The man's final proclamation got personal as the demon in him said, "I know Who You are…" Demons do have their Christology straight. Being part of the underworld of which Jesus is still Lord, the damned spirits didn't debate with the Master. They knew Who He was. We celebrate their honest and unbiased confession. Isn't that great? Demons actually told the truth. That does not mean if you encounter one they will be honest. That Christ-centered confession wasn't all. There's more.

A few chapters later, the disciples crossed the Sea of Galilee after Jesus calmed the storm. That storm got their attention and left a definite impact. They then came to the Gadarenes and a demon-possessed guy came running out of the tombs. Apparently, this guy was a handful. Let us never think we can handle a person with an unclean spirit without the help of the Lord. They couldn't tie this guy up, not even with chains. They tried, but his superhuman strength overcame the chains and shackles. All day and night, he screamed and cut himself with stones. People can open themselves to such bizarre behavior with alcohol, drugs or prohibited activities like a seance. "Demon rum" isn't called that without good reason.

This demon-possessed man's approach was different. We're told he ran and worshipped Jesus. We don't know why or exactly what that meant, but he accused Jesus saying, *"What have I to do with You, Jesus, Son of the*

Most High God? I implore You by God that You do not torment me."

Jesus asked the demon his name, not because He was looking for information but that all would see what He would do. The answer revealed there was more than one demon. They called themselves "Legion, for we are many." Rather than being sent out of the country, they begged Jesus to cast them into some nearby pigs.

Again, we see a demoniacs' knowledge of Christology. They also have an understanding of eschatology, the formal study of events explained in Scripture that happen as this world comes to a close. The demons showed true understanding of what would happen at the end of this world. They knew Who Jesus was and they knew judgement is coming. Those were true confessions. These individuals spoke the truth when confronted by Jesus or His chosen ones in ministry. When faced with the Lord Jesus Christ, they had no choice but to confess His Lordship. This is the beautiful side of such an unfortunate situation.

An interesting conclusion to this story is the people's reaction. They wanted Jesus gone; they asked Him to leave. Why would people who just saw what Jesus did want Him gone? They were fearful of losing money. He just negatively affected their economy by causing a profitable pork operation to run off a cliff. The bottom line is that even though they were ungodly people, they were afraid of righteous spiritual power and they couldn't handle Jesus disturbing their daily life. Not everyone who sees what Jesus does or hears His wisdom wants it. Jesus said there would only be a few who choose to follow Him. We should never forget that. People visit churches with great preaching all the time, yet many are not moved, not even slightly.

Aside from this example of true statements spoken by demons concerning Who Jesus was, we are also reminded that when people see what Jesus can do, they still don't want to be disturbed from their daily routine. Maybe that answers some of the disturbing things we see happening in and around churches in our day.

A final thought for this is: Let us not be shown up or embarrassed by demons who tell the truth when recognizing the Lord of Lords. That should be our privilege.

"JESUS I KNOW AND PAUL I KNOW, BUT WHO ARE YOU?"

This account describes what happens when demons recognize spiritual authority. This is not as much a statement of truth as it is an unveiling of knowledge within the spirit realm. In this case, it is again the demonic spiritual realm. This is a glimpse into the invisible spirit world and the power that is in Jesus' Name. The demon's question shows us a little known side of spiritual warfare. The fact is simple: people can be spiritually unprepared to fight a spiritual battle. This story gives us information on how and through whom the Lord's power works. This is what real spiritual warfare can look like. Most of us don't realize the physical power people have when possessed. We don't rely on movies to inform us; Scripture is clear and accurate. The problem is that people don't get information from Scripture. It is unfortunate so many choose other sources rather than simple explanations found in the Bible. We have to admit, this is an amazing story.

We'd love to have more information on what happened here but what we have, given by divine design, is all we need. The Lord knows what we need to hear so we can be prepared. The problem is, as people look for answers to life situations, Scripture is rarely considered. When information is tainted by unscriptural sources, the overall view is wrong. Such is the case with instances of demon possession. We consider a Bible story in the book of Acts. This book is the earliest historical record after the Gospels of how God's people did battle with invisible spiritual forces. Even though Scripture has proven itself, people still look elsewhere because *they don't want* Biblical explanations. This might be one of those cases.

At this early period of the church's growth and expansion, we find the Lord's chosen vessels doing the work of the Gospel.

We read about demonic activity in the Gospels. Without much background, all we know of this instance is that this man Sceva was reportedly a Jewish High Priest. His seven sons decided to follow early church patterns of exorcism. Word had got around about the effectiveness of the power of God operating through Jesus and the Apostles. Sceva's sons thought all it would take was an invocation using their names. Name dropping in a case like this doesn't work. They tried. Their formula was to expel the demon *"In the Name of Jesus Whom Paul preaches."* People knew this worked before, …but not this time. The reasons for this ineffectiveness has to do with the people trying this. There is no lack of power in the Name of Jesus as the Apostle Paul used that Name. We can do this if we know the Lord in a personal way. But when people outside the faith attempt to use the Name of Jesus, thinking it to be some lucky charm with little else needed other than dropping those names, they found it to be horribly ineffective. All we are told is that they attempted an exorcism in the Name of Jesus. They had no personal relationship with the Savior. It was this lack of relationship that prompted the demon to pronounce the truth concerning this power, *"Jesus I know and Paul I know, …"* This statement verifies who genuine disciples are. Then he asks this terrifying question: *"…but who are you?"* What happened next was horrifying.

This question reveals a serious lack of spiritual power on their part. What we read right after this is one loaded sentence describing the frightening outcome.

Remember these were *seven grown men* attempting this. There is no indication any of these were minors. The only information we have is in this one verse.

Here's the play by play and think about each fact: The man in whom was the demon, jumped *on them*, …all seven of them. This is a feat in itself. Imagine seeing this, one really hyper guy taking on seven men at once. This is not some TV wrestling match either. He then *overpowered them*, …all seven. He then *gave them such a beating* (again, all *seven*) that they ran out of the house *naked and wounded*. It is easy to read through Scriptural accounts in a superficial perfunctory fashion. That means we don't think much as we read. Most of us, unless purposely studying for an exam do this. We don't realize we are cramming for a test now. We don't know when pop quizzes come. These guys were not ready for what happened. It must have been a shock.

That is all we are told, but this is enough to go on. We know how critical it is to be spiritually prepared for any encounter. This is what we mean by saying we live in victory. When our lives are under the blood of Jesus and our sins are forgiven we are ready for anything. There is no hidden sin or anything we keep from the Lord. Something is coming; we don't know what, we don't know when. We have to be ready. Stories like this show us *what could happen*. Life as a Christian is exciting. There is power in the Name of Jesus…when you know Him.

"HAVE NOTHING TO DO WITH THIS JUST MAN"

This story unfolds during a feast where the custom was to release a prisoner. When Pilate asked, "…who shall I release," he probably asked this for political expediency. He knew it was because of the Jews' envy that they turned Jesus over to him. Pilate knew Jesus had no chance with this mob. Pilate also knew Jesus was a good Man, but not to the extent that Jesus was not only good but so much more.

Here we have a story with an amazing statement proving that Pilate was an idiot. Christians over the centuries have debated why things happened as they did during this trial. Biblical history is filled with amazing stories that make Hollywood movies look as lame as they are. Consider this: We have a warning during the worst trial in history, a message from Pilate's wife that is often overlooked. Consider how merciful God was to give this warning to someone close to the central power at the time. The Lord spoke to Pilate's wife in a dream. This is truly amazing and gracious.

All this happened as Pilate sat on his judgment seat. This was a big deal. As the scene unfolds, his wife sent that message, which is an indisputable truth: "*Have nothing to do with this just Man.*" How did she know this? Why did she feel so constrained to tell her husband? What was it that convinced her in that dream that Jesus was a just Man?

As usual, we wish we had more to go on. We'd like to know what the content of this dream was. The dream is not explained in any detail except that she suffered many things because of Jesus. We'd like to know what that means too. This sounds like what people under heavy conviction of the Holy Spirit experience. Any of us that have had bad dreams know the feeling of waking up with horrible feelings. However, when it has to do with such an event as this, well, that is something else.

In this account, we see how political pressure and a desire to please your constituents holds such influence on an individual. It almost sounds as if Pilate is trying to get Jesus released as the people clamor for His crucifixion. Then Pilate asks, sounding like an act of compassion on the Lord's behalf, *"Why, what evil has He done?"* Knowing who Pilate was and how he ruled, it is interesting that he seemed to care at all. Perhaps what his wife told him weighed on his conscience.

None of the attempts to release Jesus worked. All the events unfolded as the Lord decreed they would. Even though Jesus was sent to be a sacrifice for all mankind's sins, we wonder about God's grace, so wonderful and merciful that He would send a dream to the governor's wife warning him not to have anything to do with this "just Man."

As the people yelled for the release of the criminal Barabbas, Pilate gives in to the political pressure. Pilate saw that he could not prevail against the angry mob. Scripture states that a tumult was arising. So what does he do? He plays both sides of the issue, or so he thought. He washes his hands in front of the multitude while proclaiming he was innocent of the blood of this just "Person." What a politician! This looks like what politicians typically do in our day, as if by making statements of their noncompliance to previous decisions absolves them from any guilt. The righteous God will judge accordingly. All duplicity and deceit will eventually be exposed.

People often ignore warning signals. The Lord sends warnings because He loves us. These can come through our conscience or a direct word of warning or wisdom, if we have "ears to hear." Warnings from the Lord can also come through a prophetic voice, either at a church function or a word personally addressed to us. Much of what we understand comes from Scripture. How we process or ignore what we feel or do about this information says much about our true state of mind and spirit. It also reveals something about our destiny and the things we hold precious, whether it is love for this life or our dedication to the next, more significant life.

Pilate's wife in this Gospel narrative is a mere footnote, just another piece of the puzzle, reminding us that on Judgment Day it is possible we will be reminded of warnings or influences of the Spirit that we should have taken more seriously. There are leadings of the Spirit and warnings we might hear or observe in various ways. Let us not be so insensitive as not to hear what the Spirit is saying to the Church today. We can only wonder how things could have been different had the people in this story been more sensitive to His leading. Let it be our goal to never be insensitive when it comes to hearing what the Lord says, however so softly.

"I FIND NO FAULT IN HIM AT ALL"

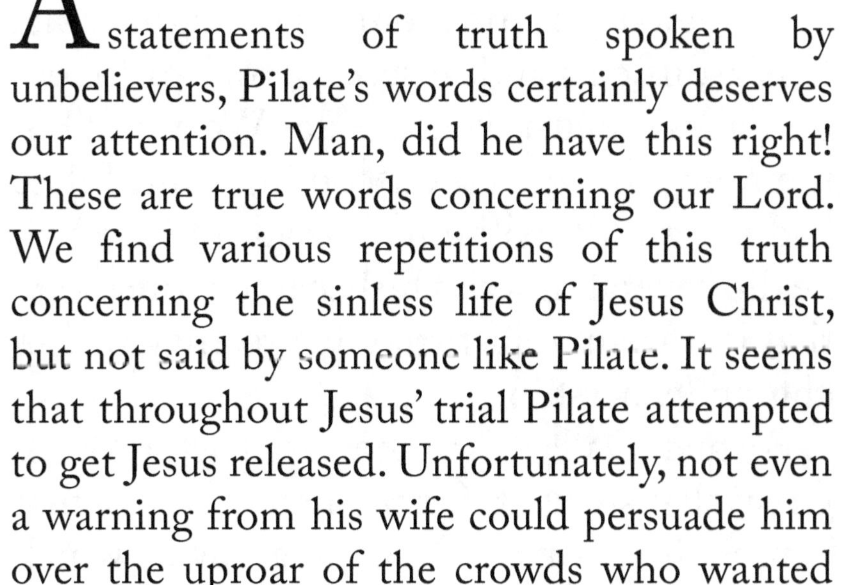

As we examine and consider these statements of truth spoken by unbelievers, Pilate's words certainly deserves our attention. Man, did he have this right! These are true words concerning our Lord. We find various repetitions of this truth concerning the sinless life of Jesus Christ, but not said by someone like Pilate. It seems that throughout Jesus' trial Pilate attempted to get Jesus released. Unfortunately, not even a warning from his wife could persuade him over the uproar of the crowds who wanted Jesus crucified. We see extreme pressure on Pilate, not from government officials, but from the organized church of the day. However,

Pontius Pilate, this ruthless political puppet had to admit there was nothing wrong with Jesus. Isn't that the truth? Cannot we agree with what Pilate said? Even he could see this in the short time he was involved with the Lord.

It is an unfortunate truth that all churches, regardless of denominational affiliation, have the potential to upset people or disappoint the masses. We see it often. Leaders say the wrong things or do the wrong things; or they don't stand up or speak out for the right thing. It is a difficult and upsetting trail to follow. Mistakes are just what we do! We are full of them and they keep on coming. But, Pilate had it right. Even he had to admit it, which he did several times as he became more aware that it was an unjust trial due to envy within church leadership.

Former Dallas First Baptist pastor W. A. Criswell's story is fitting here. At his first church in a small Oklahoma town, which also was the county seat, he would preach to farmers and ranchers bringing their goods to town. They even built him a small pavilion, a gazebo-like structure with a pulpit and shade, so he could preach without the brutal sun beating down on him. This continued for a couple of years. During his last year as pastor of that church, just on a whim, he challenged the crowds that gathered to hear him, asking, "What keeps you out of church?" These are his words.

So I said to that throng that night on the pulpit, from my little pulpit on that courthouse lawn, I said, "Why are you not in church? Why don't you go to the house of God? Why are you not numbered with the people of the Lord? Why don't you belong to God's redeemed? Why don't you go to church? Why do you separate yourself from God's people?" Now, that was a rhetorical, oratorical question in a sermon, and then I added to it, "If you can give any good reason why you separate yourself from the people of God and why you don't go to church, come up here and tell us why don't you go." Well, I never intended for anybody to come up. That was a rhetorical sermon; it was a forensic gesture. But to my amazement and surprise and astonishment and bewilderment, they came one after another. There were preachers out there. There were deacons out there, Sunday school teachers out there; every kind of a church member you can think of out there, men and women. And when I gave them that opportunity, one by one they seized it, and they came up there behind that microphone, and they poured out the most endless flood of vitriolic, caustic, castigation I ever listened to in my life! Some of those preachers would stand up there and they would describe the most terrible confrontations they had with the fellowship of deacons, or with the church membership, and why they resigned the ministry, and why they left their gospel message, and why they turned aside from the church, and why they never intended to go back. Then there were deacons there, and they came up and talked all about the preacher, and all the bad experiences that they had. And there were Sunday school teachers that came. It was awesome and terrible! After that service was over, I went home, buried my face in my hand, and said, "Lord, Lord, I can't imagine my making a mistake like that. O Lord, how did I ever get into that? It was terrible!" I can make the biggest mistakes, and that was one of them. Well, as I said, that's been over forty years ago. I have thought of that night a thousand, thousand times. I have reviewed what those preachers said as they castigated the church, what those deacons said as they castigated the preachers, what those people said as they found fault with the church and why they weren't ever going back. I have reviewed that a thousand times, and gradually there came into my heart a tremendous and convicting observation: they had much to say against the preacher, much to say against the deacon, much to say against the church, much to say against the people, but I happened finally to realize not one, not one in all of that throng, not one ever said a word against the Lord Jesus Christ. "For I find in Him no fault at all."

We have to admit there are problems in churches today and there always have been. Friction and interpersonal issues constantly challenge and test our faith. Yet we keep on regardless of the distractions within the church we attend. It is a struggle for sure but well worth the effort. We know why we are there and for Whose sake and glory.

People in every church have the potential to be messed up. We are imperfect in all our ways, but the Lord is not. Ghandi's testimony was that he'd have been a Christian *if it weren't for Christians*. Yes, we have problems but the Lord does not. No matter what bad things have happened to you in association with any church, you have to admit it never was the Lord's fault. Because in Him, that is in Christ, rightly preached, even the most sarcastic and caustic person cannot find any fault in Him still. The truth from Pilate's unsanctified lips still rings true! Blessed be the Name of all names. There is indeed, no fault in Him at all.

"CAIAPHAS' PROPHESY ABOUT JESUS' DEATH"

It is not uncommon to read in the Gospels that so many people were against Jesus. No matter what He did or said, there were those who found something wrong with Him, even though Pilate recognized there was no fault in Him. Making this account even more surprising was the fact that Lazarus was just raised from the dead. How can anyone come against something like that? Even with such an indisputable miracle, Jesus still had His unrelenting enemies. This proves that rejecting the Lord Jesus is not a decision made with only a logical or intellectual basis.

There must be some spiritual impulse to cause such wrong thinking.

Jesus' enemies' mindset was usually based on political loyalties, religious pride, and the Jews' hatred for Roman oppression. As a result, their plan was lame as they said, "*If we let Him alone like this, everyone will believe in Him and the Romans will come and take away both our place and nation.*" Notice this bizarre fact: They weren't concerned with eternal matters or even the fact that Lazarus was raised from the dead! That remarkable miracle didn't matter as much as their political concerns. What kind of people are we observing here? They are people just like us. People still do self-serving deeds in the darkness while ignoring or rejecting God's gracious Light.

The statement made by Caiaphas is striking indeed. Being the High Priest, he had considerable clout. Thus, he begins with an authoritative tone, "*You know nothing at all...*" Don't you just love it when some blowhard in charge begins his discourse with the words "Hey, you're all a bunch of idiots!"

We are not sure why Caiaphas began like that. Pride usually plays a part. It was probably because he saw *what he thought* was an easy way out of an uncomfortable situation for their people. However, what he did expound and pontificate on was exactly right.

The truth, despite the fact that the priest spoke disrespectfully about the Lord, may have started off as blasphemy but God used his words to effectively preach the eternal Gospel. And get this: All this happened unwittingly to the priest *even as he was doing the talking*. You have to appreciate the Lord's sense of humor. Whether it's a jackass or a High Priest doing the talking, God's will shall be done.

The priest began with the practical angle, or so it seemed. It would be advantageous, the enemies thought, for this "one man" to be sacrificed for the good of the nation. Evidently, this was their political approach to fix the situation. The High Priest rambled on how if they got rid of Jesus, the people would have rest. How wrong that was! But the priest wasn't finished. If only that information was recorded, we'd be in the dark about what happened. Luke gives us the sanctified commentary on the why and how of what was said. Luke tells us Caiaphas said what was spoken *not of his own authority but because he was the High Priest that year*. That being his official function, he was speaking as an oracle or spokesman for the Most High God. This was part of his spiritual function as High Priest. Whether he knew what was happening or not, he spoke the truth for God. That's what happened! Jesus was so much more than just a man. Therefore, God spoke truth through an unbelieving person who happened to be in an official religious capacity.

Isn't it amazing such a thing as that could happen? Didn't the priest hear himself? Couldn't he process what he just said? Maybe he heard his own words in a superficial fashion, but he was not able to "hear" with those crucial "ears-to-hear" of which Jesus often spoke. This ability to truly "hear" what the Spirit of God says to His Church is something we get from the Lord Himself. Unfortunately, for spiritual leadership at that occasion there was little, if any, "hearing" or discernment. There may have been some, but not much considering the great number of people who heard and saw what happened. They entirely missed the big picture.

Luke's historical explanation reveals the words of the High Priest had an amazing redemptive effect. Most of the people instigating this trouble were only concerned with temporary issues. Their political and religious issues were at stake. Luke's record went further including the fact that Jesus would have to die, but not only for Israel at that historical time. This death-to-top-all-deaths would include salvation for all God's chosen ones who would eventually believe and be saved through His Name. It didn't matter how far they were scattered abroad or whether or not they were born. This is good news for everyone, regardless of when we were born. *It means glorious salvation, total forgiveness and redemption for whosoever believes on Jesus.* We amen this unbelieving High Priest as he was right on target.

We should understand how amazing the High Priest's words were. The religious leaders wanted to get rid of Jesus. He was bad for their religious franchise. Jesus was having a negative effect on political and business matters regarding the nation of Israel at that time. The leaders wanted Him gone and that was soon to happen. All this happened by people inadvertently acting as if by their own accord, yet fulfilling the will of God. What an accomplishment! This is the greatest work of redemption, *available to whomever believes it!* We can say together what is also sung in many churches today: **"Our God is an awesome God, He reigns from Heaven above, with wisdom, power and love, Our God is an awesome God."**

"HE SAVED OTHERS, HIMSELF HE CANNOT SAVE"

This may be the most incredible and touching statement considered in this volume. Understanding redemption has never been easy. The substitutionary sacrifice of Christ seems ludicrous to people without grace and faith to believe. The world may see it like CNN founder Ted Turner who reportedly once said, "Christianity is a religion for losers. I don't want anybody dying for me." It was later reported that Turner revised his statements. I hope he did. God's grace is available.

There is no doubt Jesus left His mark on this world. Most civilized populations commemorate His work on the cross and His resurrection from the dead. Our calendars testify to His impact, "Anno Domini" (AD). We know this means, "The year of our Lord," even though heathens hate to admit it. Some have recently proposed changing that by calling our age "CE," meaning "common era" so that unbelievers would not be offended. What about all of us who would be greatly offended by that insensitive secular move? AD precedes the date where CE comes after it, but they both refer to the same beginning. There's nothing common about our Lord, but He certainly is current. He accomplished this great work on the cross and He is coming back to finish it. No one will ever undo what our Lord did for us, whether the calendar agrees or not.

Picture the setting of this Biblical account with cynics, and general unbelief throughout apostate Israel. The people were in no spiritual condition to receive their King. They did not recognize Him when they talked to Him face to face.

This scene is the crucifixion, where Scripture records that spiritually dead worldlings sat down and watched Jesus there (v. 36). The accusation we consider, true as it was, would not sink in for the world to know for a while. This statement is possibly the greatest saying describing our Lord's work of redemption. This is even more startling when we realize it was said by unbelievers as they mocked the Lord. Oh, how the Jews hated that sign over our Lord in three languages. That did not change the truth of its message acknowledging His glorious title. He was and still is the King of the Jews. Even Pilate, sounding like he was fed up with their complaints, shot back with: "*What I have written I have written.*" Jesus is still the King of Kings. Whosoever believes on His substitutionary work that He did for us is granted repentance unto life. This Savior and His plan of salvation are so much bigger than we realize.

We remember the ancient cynics as they sat in a garbage dump outside Jerusalem, our Lord hanging between two thieves. Casual observers shook their heads in disbelief while one among the chief priests, scribes, and elders spoke these words. *What they said was meant in the most sarcastic hateful mockery and yet tells us exactly what and how He accomplished this in the greatest example of love.* These words describe the most excellent and glorious spiritual truth of redemption even though it was unknown to those who said it.

We note their faulty criteria when compared to the genuineness of His claims being the Son of God. It did not make sense to them.

Another example of blind understanding is found in verse 40 which states their objection to His preaching concerning Himself: "*So you will destroy the temple and build it again in three days.*" Wrong! How smart we think we are. They didn't know what temple Jesus was talking about. The jeers to save Himself and come down from the cross were possible, but Jesus wouldn't stoop to their level to satisfy their curiosity. He could have called 12 legions (6 thousand each) of angels (72 thousand) to come rescue Him, but that would end all chances for salvation. This travesty of His death only *seemed* to end His life, *but it was temporary.* The temple, meaning His body, would be gloriously rebuilt as God reversed the curse of death on His Son. Jesus laid

His life down with this amazing miracle in mind—*that He might take it up again.*

In verses 41-43, mocking His kingship, the crowd commanded Jesus to come down from the cross. In these words, their ignorance shined and unbelievers today ignorantly follow. The statement was never more true than from the lips of religious mockers: ***"He saved others…"*** They mocked without believing. We know if they believed they would not have mocked. The truth of His sacrifice is brought out by unbelievers in vivid clarity. It was absolutely true that He saved others and in order to accomplish that… ***Himself He could not save.*** This sacrifice for mankind, so complete and effective could not be done any other way: *He could not save Himself.* What is the perfect sacrifice if not His life? Herein lies the truth of our salvation.

Note well the crowd's bold assertions spoken in ignorance. The lost world still believes like this. They want everything they can get while living a self-indulgent life. No one gets it both ways. What is amazing is that people can speak absolute truth without knowing what they just said. Such is the case here.

There are related thoughts for Christian fruitfulness is this account: If you save yourself, you won't be effectual in anyone else's salvation. If you live to please your own wants, there is no practical spiritual use in your life. Jesus said: "*If you find your life, you lose it.*" You don't have what it takes if you live only for yourself! Dietrich Bonhoeffer, a Lutheran pastor killed by the Nazis said, "*When Christ calls a man, he bids him come and die.*" Bonhoeffer knew the cost of discipleship. If we save ourselves and live only for our pleasures, we are of little-to-no use in God's kingdom. We must honor our Savior by measuring up to what He requires and deserves in His disciples. Matthew 16: 24-27 states the following:

Then Jesus said to His disciples, "*If anyone wishes to come after Me, he must deny himself, and take up his cross and follow Me. For whoever wishes to save his life will lose it; but whoever loses his life for My sake will find it. For what will it profit a man if he gains the whole world and forfeits his soul? Or what will a man give in exchange for his soul? For the Son of Man is going to come in the glory of His Father with His angels, and will then repay every man according to his deeds."*

Believe on Jesus; die to yourself. Live your life for Christ alone. Follow Him in this pattern for sacrifice. Oh, what a Savior!

9 781950 947294